After I Die

*What My Executor
Will Need to Know*

Fran Stewart

After I Die

© Fran Stewart

ISBN: 978-1-951368-50-0

This book was printed in the United States of America

Books by Fran Stewart

Fiction:

<u>**The Biscuit McKee Mystery Series:**</u>

Orange as Marmalade
Yellow as Legal Pads
Green as a Garden Hose
Blue as Blue Jeans
Indigo as an Iris
Violet as an Amethyst
Gray as Ashes
Red as a Rooster
Black as Soot
Pink as a Peony
White as Ice

A Slaying Song Tonight

Turnaround (coming soon)

<u>**The ScotShop Mysteries**</u>

A Wee Murder in My Shop
A Wee Dose of Death
A Weee Homicide in the Hotel

Poetry:

Resolution

For Children:

As Orange As Marmalade/
    Tan naranja como Mermelada
        (a bilingual book)

Non-Fiction:

From The Tip of My Pen: a manual for writers

BeesKnees #1: A Beekeeping Memoir (#1 of 6 volumes)
BeesKnees #2: A Beekeeping Memoir (#2 of 6 volumes)
BeesKnees #3: A Beekeeping Memoir (#3 of 6 volumes)
BeesKnees #4: A Beekeeping Memoir (#4 of 6 volumes)
BeesKnees #5: A Beekeeping Memoir (#5 of 6 volumes)
BeesKnees #6: A Beekeeping Memoir (#6 of 6 volumes)

Clear as Mud
Clearly Me
Crystal Clear

After I Die: What My Executor Will Need to Know

TABLE OF CONTENTS

NOTE: Item numbers are easy to spot in the right-hand margins

NOTE: Extra thanks go to my very helpful pre-readers, Veronica Lowe, Karen Krotz, and Marcia Dunscomb for their suggestions on ways I could streamline the text, make the lists more understandable, and cut out the excess verbiage. If I've goofed anywhere, it's not their fault!

Chapter 1 – How This Came About

This all started when the husband of a friend of mine died unexpectedly, and she was left with a mountain of missing information. Where were his bank accounts? What about insurance? Was there a list of his valuable assets (not just money, but collectibles and family heirlooms)?

When I mentioned all this to my daughter, who will be my executor, she said, "Mom, would you put together a list of the five most important things I have to do right after you die? I wouldn't even know where to start."

So I went onto DuckDuckGo and searched for important things to do after somebody dies. The most helpful list was at the AARP website. I'm grateful to the people who compiled it, and I've incorporated many of their ideas into this book.

BUT it turns out there aren't FIVE most important things to do. There are way more than that, so my five-item list turned into six pages. And then there was all the other stuff that will need to be handled—another eight or nine pages.

I did all this searching and sorting and asking so my daughter wouldn't have to reinvent the wheel. When I told my friend about THE LIST, she asked me to make it into a book.

Voilá! Here it is.

> —Fran Stewart
> from my house beside a creek
> on the other side of Hog Mountain GA
> December 2023

p.s. You'll probably notice as you go through this process that I've written this book from the viewpoint of someone who lives alone in a house. Your circumstances may be different; if you **rent** an apartment, or you live with a **roommate**, a **spouse**, a **grandchild**—then you'll ignore the instructions to "sell my house" or to "get someone to clean out the fridge." Just use your common sense and you'll be okay.

8

Chapter 2 –Before You Start Filling in the Blanks:
This is Fran's note <u>to the one who's going to</u> <u>pass this info on to an executor</u>

I've written all these instructions in first person, as if you're simply leaving a shopping list for the one who's going to take care of things after you croak, whether that's twenty years from now or just around the corner.

Fill out as many lines as you can. **Do it in pencil in case you need to update the book later.** It'll take you some time, but just think of how much it will help your executor when the time comes. There are a lot of check boxes here and there. If the answer is No, just cross out that area so they don't spend time wondering if you forgot to fill in some of the lines. If you need more lines, you can write on the facing page.

You do have a will, don't you? A current will? If not, that's your very first job. Believe me, dying without one is not something anybody should consider (especially if you have minor children!) Some people want a do-it-yourself will from a form they found online, some may want one that's just the bare bones, while others may go for a will that's more complicated than an orchestral score. That's up to you. Just be sure you have one that will be considered legal in your state. And be sure it's one that will protect your heirs. If, for instance, all the money for the support of your minor children is tied up in trusts, your spouse (and the children) might be left close to starving. I strongly suggest that you work with an attorney to navigate those waters before you die.

Making a will doesn't mean you're going to die soon. It means that whenever you do get around to dying, the people you leave behind won't resent your lack of consideration. You should consider signing a power of attorney (POA), a health care power of attorney, and a living will. If you don't, your loved ones could be left in legal or medical limbo.

- A **power of attorney** allows the person you've designated to act on your behalf in case you're off on a long vacation or incapacitated in some way. They can transact business for you if you can't do it yourself. Obviously, you'll want to choose someone you trust.
- A **health care power of attorney** lets you appoint someone to make medical decisions on your behalf if and when you can't do it yourself.
- A **living will**, which may or may not be incorporated into your health care power of attorney, lets you decide which life-sustaining procedures (if any) may be used to prolong your life when it's been medically determined that there's no hope of sustaining life without intervention.

If you have a Do Not Resuscitate (DNR) order but you want to donate organs, you might have to indicate that the desire to donate supersedes the DNR, since the heart may have to be kept beating to keep your organs alive until they can be removed. You'll need to talk to your lawyer about this when you draw up your will.

Something you can do now is to ask a neighbor if they'd be willing to stay at your house when it's time for your funeral. Then you'll list them in Item #17. Why? Because some scumbags search the obits for funeral notices, find out your address, and bring a truck or van to clean out your house while everyone you love is attending your funeral.

Please note: if you have dependents with special needs, it is far beyond the scope of this book to provide the questions for you to answer. You may need to set up trust funds or arrange for designated caregivers. The possibilities are myriad. That's why I've left blank pages at the end, where you can record these special

considerations. Please know that I honor your commitment.

Once you've filled this book out as completely as you can, **go over it with your executor** so they'll understand what's going on, and so they'll appreciate how nice you're being to them! This will give them a chance to ask questions (and you may need to go back and revise things here and there). Also, at this time, you should **give them a key to your house** if they don't already have one.

I strongly recommend that you **keep this book (once it's filled out) in your safe deposit box or home safe**, since it would be a gold mine to anyone who had unauthorized access to it. **Just be sure your executor will have immediate access to that safe or deposit box and knows how to get into it!**

Please know that I'm proud of you for taking these steps to help your executor be as prepared as possible. I wish you well.

    --Fran

Take the first step now and begin gathering this information together.

Something to think about:

If you have secrets, as many people do, rest assured that they are likely to be uncovered at some point after your death. There is space in any life for privacy, but secrets tend to be toxic and may bring pain to your survivors.

You might want to consider these four things now:

- What those secrets are

- What disruption their discovery will cause

- What to do about revealing them before you die, or

- How to leave an explanation so your family isn't torn apart.

As I say, this is just something for you to think about.

Chapter 3 – Before You Start Executing This Will
This is Fran's note to the executor.

The person who asked you to serve as executor is trying with this little book to make things a whole lot easier for you. This is their gift to you. If you have a chance to, please thank them for being so considerate!

There are checkboxes for each item where you can note that you've completed that item (and the date it was completed). This is important because if you're doing this while you're still stunned by the death, you may not remember whether you notified this person or took care of that item. With the checkboxes, you won't have to worry about missing something.

Also, there are checkboxes in the index. If you check those when you've completed them, you won't have to scroll through the book looking for items you might have missed. Any that are unchecked, you can go quickly to that item number.

Being an executor almost always comes at a time when you're trying to deal with your own grief. It can be an exhausting and time-consuming process. If you need to consider talking to a **bereavement counselor**, rest assured that many people have benefitted from being able to talk it all out. You'll be under a lot of pressure to get all the things on this list accomplished – but you don't need to fall apart while you're doing it, so take a deep breath, remember the good times, take some time to relax, journal if you need to, and ask for help if you need it. **In other words, take care of yourself**.

I wish you a journey in which you learn a lot and experience a great deal of satisfaction for a job well done.

    --Fran

Chapter 4 – Let's Get Started
This is a note from
me
to my executor

My dear executor,

You're going to need to know an awful lot about me before I croak, and you're going to need to take care of a lot of details afterwards. But I trust you. SO, here's a brief overview of what to expect. Keep in mind that this book cannot possibly cover everything you'll need to know, and

IT'S NOT MEANT TO REPLACE GOOD LEGAL ADVICE.

But what's in here should be a big help.

I've filled out as many blanks and check boxes as I can, starting with the basic info in chapter 5.

The other chapters get into the nitty-gritty, step-by-step details of
- things to do right away,
- things that can wait a couple of weeks, and
- things that you'll get around to sometime or other.

Feel free to make notes and jot down reminders in the margins.

I assure you that ☐ I will ☐ I won't come back to haunt you if you end up doing things slightly differently than I've asked.

_____
Signed

_____
Date

Note from Fran*: Sign it in ink but put the date in pencil. You'll probably make plenty of changes over the next few years.*

Chapter 5 – Where to Find All My Important Legal Stuff

This is a shopping list that will help you find all my important documents after I'm dead. My job is to complete it. Thoroughly.

Basic Info: **1**

My legal name: _____

My birthdate: _____ Mother's maiden name: _____

My birthplace: _____

Birth certificate location: _____

My phone number: _____ (password/passcode) _____

My social security number: _____

My current address: _____

City/State/ZIP _____

☐ Own   ☐ Rent   ☐ Rest Home   ☐ Care Facility   ☐ Other

List details here:

DNR directive: **2**

☐ I have   ☐ I do not have one.

Location: _____

Sometimes—especially if you call 911—first responders may try to revive me.
Be sure you have my DNR handy. Note: Some people keep it on their fridge door. If I am an organ donor (see Item #10) the donor status must supercede the DNR.

Passwords: **3**

My phone password (you'll need it right away) is _____

☐ I do not have a password list, so a lot of things are going to fall through the cracks.

☐ I do have a list of passwords. It's located:

_____

☐ I sort of made notes about my passwords here and there. Here are some hopefully helpful suggestions about where to find them:

_____

Citizenship papers: **4**

☐ I do   ☐ I don't   have these.

Location   _____

Adoption records: **5**

☐ I do   ☐ I don't   have these.

Location   _____

Religious Community: **6**

☐ I do   ☐ I don't   have a religious community

What it is: _____

Contact person:_____

   Phone: _____

   Email   _____

   Street: _____

   City/State/ZIP   _____

Marital status: **7**

☐ Single   ☐ Married   (number of marriages:_____)

Legal name of current spouse or partner: _____

  Phone # _____

Marriage certificate location   _____

☐ We don't have pre-nuptial or post-nuptial agreements

☐ We do have them. They're located: _____

Previous spouse(s)   **8**
☐ Don't bother to contact them.
☐ Do contact them:

#1 Name: _____

Phone: _____

Email   _____

Street: _____

City/State/ZIP   _____

☐ Completed
Date completed_____

#2 Name: _____

Phone: _____

Email   _____

Street: _____

City/State/ZIP   _____

☐ Completed
Date completed_____

Location of divorce decree(s) _____

My employer (*if applicable*)   **9**

☐ Contacted

Date completed_____

Company: _____

Contact person   _____

Phone: _____

Email   _____

Street: _____

City/State/ZIP   _____

Date(s) of employment _____

Note: The heirs may have benefits due them.

Chapter 6 – What to Do Immediately After I Die
First – take a deep breath.

- Am I an **organ donor**? ☐ Yes ☐ No   **10**
- Am I a **bone marrow donor**? ☐ Yes ☐ No

    Note: Bone marrow donation is permitted only by people who are **18-40 years of age**.

- Get an **official declaration of death**.   **11**

If I die anywhere other than a hospital or under hospice care, you'll have a hard time getting an official declaration, since it must be signed by a doctor, so call 911 to take my body to a hospital, which will then issue the declaration. But keep in mind that if I die at home, there's no need to call 911 right away (unless I've chosen to be an organ donor). You might want to have someone make sure my body is lying flat before the joints become stiff. This rigor mortis begins sometime during the first few hours after death. If my death was sudden or unexpected, a coroner or medical examiner might be required to attend the scene of death. The rules may vary from state to state, but the first responders should be able to tell you what applies. **(See item #42 about ordering copies.)**

- Keep a detailed list of every single cent you spend in doing this executor stuff.   **12**

You are entitled to repayment for it all. If you have questions about how to do it, ask my lawyer (even though they'll probably charge to give you an answer).

☐ Started

Date completed_____

Children / Dependents   **13**

I ☐ do ☐ do not have **adult** children.

I ☐ do ☐ do not have **minor** children or other dependents.

Get my kids to a safe place with a trustworthy adult who can care for them for 24–48 hours.

I ☐ am ☐ am not their legal guardian

Their legal guardian is _____ / ph. _____

<u>**Child or Dependent's Name**</u>	<u>**Birthdate**</u>

* _____   _____

* _____   _____

* _____   _____

* _____   _____

Call the funeral home to collect my body   **14**

Name: _____

Phone: _____   Email _____

Street: _____

City/State/ZIP _____

☐ Contacted
Date completed_____

Note: The county coroner or 911 can also transport the body for you. Otherwise, you'll need to call a funeral home or crematorium to do this. These businesses are legally required to tell you how much their services will cost, so ask and write down the price. If I have a pre-paid burial policy, transportation costs should already be covered.

Burial Policy and Burial Instructions   **15**

* I have a burial policy   ☐ Yes   ☐ No

   If yes, the policy paperwork is located: _____

* I want to be   ☐ buried   ☐ cremated

* I want   ☐ embalmed   ☐ natural (green) burial with no embalming

* I want   ☐ open casket   ☐ closed casket

* I own a cemetery plot   ☐ Yes   ☐ No

Cemetery: _____ Plot # _____

Phone: _____

Email _____

Street: _____

City/State/ZIP _____

Note:

Secure my house and car (be sure they're locked) and get someone to clean up anything that's likely to stink later: **16**

- Empty the fridge

- Clean the bathroom(s)

- Deal with dirty laundry (be sure to check the washer)

☐ Done

Date completed_____

Does anyone else have a house key or car key?   ☐ Yes ☐ No

If so, who is it? _____ / _____

Do I need a code of some sort to get into my house? ☐ Yes ☐ No

Who knows it? _____

_____

Call these people in this order   family / closest friends / other / neighbors   **17**

Family:

Name	Phone	
_____ / _____	☐
_____ / _____	☐
_____ / _____	☐
_____ / _____	☐
_____ / _____	☐
_____ / _____	☐

☐ All Contacted

Date completed_____

My closest friends:

Name	Phone	
_____ / _____	☐
_____ / _____	☐
_____ / _____	☐

☐ All Contacted

Date completed_____

Other people who might need to know immediately. There's a section later on other people to notify after you've planned a funeral/memorial service.

Name	Phone
_____	/ _____ ☐
_____	/ _____ ☐
_____	/ _____ ☐

☐ All Contacted

Date completed_____

Neighbors:

Note: The starred one is somebody who's willing to keep an eye on my house during the funeral service and the others are ones who will watch over it until it's sold.

Name	Phone
** _____	/ _____ ☐
_____	/ _____ ☐
_____	/ _____ ☐

☐ All Contacted

Date completed_____

Begin to plan the funeral / end of life service   **18**

- I ☐ do ☐ do not   expect you to go broke putting on my funeral

- I ☐ do ☐ don't   want a fancy newspaper obituary (which can cost several hundred dollars).

- I ☐ have ☐ haven't   written my own **obituary**.

    If I have, you'll find it here: _____

    If I haven't, get somebody who's good with words to write it.

☐ Contacted

Date completed_____

If you want to plan a memorial service separate from the funeral, there's information about that in item #69.

I ☐ have   ☐ have not   received awards that I'd like mentioned:

_____

_____

_____

In lieu of flowers, feel free to donate to _____

Arrange for: **pall bearers** (if applicable):

Name	Phone	
• _____	/ _____	☐
• _____	/ _____	☐
• _____	/ _____	☐
• _____	/ _____	☐
• _____	/ _____	☐
• _____	/ _____	☐

☐ Completed

Date completed_____

Arrange for someone to conduct the service

This is who I'd prefer:

_____ / _____ ☐

☐ Contacted
Date completed_____

Arrange for people to deliver comments or the eulogy (or sing)

_____ / _____ ☐

_____ / _____ ☐

_____ / _____ ☐

☐ Completed
Date completed_____

Note: Traditional funerals are usually a **MAJOR expense**, so be very careful what you plan. It's important not to be guilted into choosing the most expensive options.

More about the funeral / end of life service:

I kind of hope you ☐ open the service to everyone ☐ keep it family only

I ☐ will ☐ won't   haunt you if you ignore these wishes.

I ☐ have ☐ haven't   put together some requests about my funeral service.

You'll find them here: _____

I ☐ am ☐ am not   eligible for military honors at my funeral.

If I am, then you'll need to arrange that, but you'll need a death certificate and my military enlistment or discharge papers. Any funeral director can help you arrange for an honor guard.

Location of military documents: _____

Application form: https://www.usa.gov/military-funeral-honors

Contact Person   _____

Phone   _____

☐ Completed

Date completed_____

Arrange a wake or an "after the funeral get-together" if you want to.   **19**

If you're planning to have a memorial service (either right before or right after the funeral, or even a lot later), you can send an email blast (by blind copy please! Protect their contact info) to everybody on my contact list.

Here's the general wording for you to use. You can revise it any way you want to.

= = = = = = = = = = = = =

I'm the daughter/son/wife/husband/whatever of _____, who died peacefully on _____. I went through her/his contact list and found your information. Here is the obituary:

Cut and paste it here

There will be a memorial service on _____(date) at _____(place)

We plan to celebrate her/his life. I hope you can join us either in person or in spirit.

Your name here.

Sent by blind copy to protect your privacy.

= = = = = = = = = =   ☐ Completed

Date completed_____

Naturally, you can change the wording of this any way you want to.

Arrange care for my ☐ cat ☐ dog ☐ bird ☐ fish ☐ plants ☐ other   **20**

Here's what I'd prefer if possible:

☐ Completed

Date completed_____

Decide which **utilities/services** need to be canceled immediately and which need to be kept   **21**
for now.

☐ electricity

Company_____ Account #_____

☐ Completed

Date completed_____

☐ gas

Company_____ Account #_____

☐ Completed

Date completed_____

☐ phone

Company_____ Account #_____

☐ Completed

Date completed_____

☐ cable

    Company _____ Account # _____

                                 ☐ Completed
                                 Date completed _____

☐ other

    Company _____ Account # _____

                                 ☐ Completed
                                 Date completed _____

Forward all my mail to your house for up to a year.   **22**

    You can do this at USPS.com

    You'll learn a lot from the mail I get. I may have skipped something in these lists, so check my mail to be sure everything's covered.

                                 ☐ Completed
                                 Date completed _____

Go through **my home safe** or **safe deposit box**   **23**

    (You won't be able to get into a safe deposit box until after you have a death certificate

    unless you're a co-signer).

    Do I have a safe deposit box?   ☐ Yes   ☐ No

    Bank/Branch: _____ / _____ Box number: _____

    Key's location _____

I ☐ have ☐ have not   made a list of everything in my safe deposit box.

The list is located _____

                                   ☐ Completed
                                 Date completed _____

Do I have a home safe: ☐ Yes   ☐ No

Location _____

Access information (or where to find that info) _____

I ☐ have ☐ have not   made a list of everything in there.

The list is located _____

☐ Completed
Date completed_____

Make sure you have my will, POA, and other pertinent documents   **24**

- **Will/Living Trust**   **25**
   Do I have either one?   ☐ Yes   ☐ No

Location of original document(s): _____

☐ Found

Date(s) created:_____/_____/_____

Law firm that prepared document(s) _____

Contact person   _____

Phone: _____

Email _____

Street: _____

City/State/ZIP _____

- **Power of Attorney**   **26**

    I have one   ☐ Yes   ☐ No

    Location of original document: _____

    ☐ Found

    Name of person given the power to act on my behalf _____

    Phone: _____

    Email   _____

    Street: _____

    City/State/ZIP   _____

    ☐ Found

- **Health Care Power of Attorney / Living Will**   **27**

    Do I have either one?   ☐ Yes   ☐ No

    Location of original document(s):   _____

    ☐ Found

    Note: Tell my beneficiaries that they're in my will—but don't get their hopes too high. They can't legally receive their inheritance until it goes through probate.

Contact these businesses:

My current lawyer   **28**

Is this the same attorney who drafted my will?   ☐ Yes   ☐ No

Here's the current lawyer's contact info (if different from Item 25).

Name: _____

Phone: _____

Email _____

Street: _____

City/State/ZIP _____

☐ Contacted

Date completed_____

Primary Care Doc: _____   **29**

Phone: _____

Email _____

Street: _____

City/State/ZIP _____

☐ Contacted

Date completed_____

My Accountant / Tax Returns   **30**

Ask them to let you know what they'll need in order to complete my taxes for the previous year and the current one.

Name: _____

Phone: _____

Email _____

Street: _____

City/State/ZIP _____

☐ Contacted

Date completed_____

Location of my tax records if not with an accountant: _____

_____

Note: Probate court may require up to three years of tax returns. For the current year, you must report all income through the date of death and file the return by the usual April deadline.

Social Security 800-772-1213 (they will notify Medicare if necessary).   **31**

Generally, the funeral home will notify SSA, but double-check to be sure it's been done since it is the survivor's responsibility to be sure they've been notified.

You will probably have to arrange a later appointment to deliver a death certificate to them. This can take quite a while.

☐ Notified

Date completed_____

Insurance Policies

Consider contacting them now, but you will have to provide a death certificate at a later date.

Life Insurance: Do I have any policies insuring my life, or do I own any policies on someone else's life?

☐ Yes   ☐ No   **32**

Name/Policy #: _____

Phone: _____

Email _____

Street: _____

City/State/ZIP _____

☐ Contacted

Date completed_____

Do I have primary medical insurance   ☐ Yes   ☐ No   **33**

Name/Policy #: _____

Phone: _____

Email _____

Street: _____

City/State/ZIP _____

☐ Contacted

Date completed_____

Secondary insurance policy?   ☐ Yes   ☐ No   **34**

Name/Policy #:   _____

Phone: _____

Email   _____

Street: _____

City/State/ZIP   _____

☐ Contacted

Date completed_____

Long Time Care Insurance?   ☐ Yes   ☐ No   **35**

Name/Policy #:   _____

Phone: _____

Email   _____

Street: _____

City/State/ZIP   _____

☐ Contacted

Date completed_____

Intensive Care Policy   ☐ Yes   ☐ No   **36**

Note: If I've been in intensive care, be sure to file a claim.

Company _____ policy #_____

Agent's name _____

Phone: _____

Email _____

Street: _____

City/State/ZIP _____

☐ Cancelled

Date completed_____

Any other insurance   ☐ Yes   ☐ No   **37**

Name/Policy #: _____

Phone: _____

Email _____

Street: _____

City/State/ZIP _____

☐ Contacted

Date completed_____

Fill out a Deceased Do Not Contact form to stop junk mail   **38**

https://www.ims-dm.com/cgi/ddnc.php

Cancel automatic monthly donations to these organizations   **39**

<u>Name</u>   <u>Phone</u>

_____ / _____

Website or email: _____

☐ Cancelled

Date completed_____

_____ / _____

Website or email: _____

☐ Cancelled

Date completed_____

_____ / _____

Website or email: _____

☐ Cancelled

Date completed_____

_____ / _____

Website or email: _____

☐ Cancelled

Date completed_____

Cancel automatic monthly donations to these organizations (continued)

Name   Phone

_____ / _____

Website or email: _____

☐ Cancelled

Date completed_____

Cancel automatic yearly renewals for these organizations, such as my phone service,   **40**
streaming services, newspaper, cable and internet, and ongoing home delivery services.
Be sure not to cancel ones that may need to remain active for a while.

Business Name   Phone

_____ / _____

Website or email: _____

☐ Cancelled

Date completed_____

_____ / _____

Website or email: _____

☐ Cancelled

Date completed_____

_____ / _____

Website or email: _____

☐ Cancelled

Date completed_____

Cancel automatic yearly renewals for these organizations (continued)

<u>Business Name</u>   <u>Phone</u>

_____ / _____

Website or email: _____

☐ Cancelled

Date completed_____

_____ / _____

Website or email: _____

☐ Cancelled

Date completed_____

Consider hiring an attorney (mine or yours) to help distribute the money.   **41**

Name: _____

Phone: _____

Email   _____

Street: _____

City/State/ZIP   _____

☐ Contacted

Date of 1st meeting_____

Date completed_____

Chapter 7 – What to Do Several Weeks After I Die

(because you'll need death certificates for most of these things)

Get at least 15 (maybe more) certified copies of death certificate.   **42**

The funeral home should be able to order them for you. Or you can order them from the county's Vital Statistics Office (search for county court probate death certificates). NOTE: They won't be available until at least 2 weeks after my death. Sometimes it takes 4 to 6 weeks. Be patient.

☐ Ordered

Date received_____

Note: The cost of these certificates vary a great deal from state to state. In Georgia, for instance, the first certificate will cost you $25. Additional certificates you order at that same time are $5 each.

If you run out of certificates, though, and need to order more, the first one will again cost you $25, plus $5 for others. So it's better to order too many up front.

Begin to put together a list of assets.   **43**

Many of them are listed here in this book, but you'll need the actual figures as of the date of my death. This is usually required by the probate court. You may have to hire an appraiser for physical objects in the home. See item #89

☐ Completed

Date completed_____

Be sure mortgage, taxes, car loan and necessary utilities continue to be paid while the estate   **44**
is being settled. Here's information about my real property:

Property Deeds / Mortgage(s)   **45**

My primary residence? ☐ Yes ☐ No   I have an outstanding mortgage ☐ Yes ☐ No

Location of deed(s): _____

Address: _____

Mortgage on this property: company: _____

loan # _____   monthly payment $_____

due on _____   ☐ automatic debit   ☐ paid by check
         date

                                          ☐ Arranged

                                          Date completed_____

. . . .

Address of real estate #2 I own: _____

Is this a rental property?   ☐ Yes   ☐ No
I have an outstanding mortgage   ☐ Yes   ☐ No

Mortgage on this property: company: _____

loan # _____   monthly payment $_____

due on _____   ☐ automatic debit   ☐ paid by check
         date

                                          ☐ Arranged

                                          Date completed_____

. . . .

Address of real estate #3 I own: _____

Is this a rental property?   ☐ Yes   ☐ No
I have an outstanding mortgage   ☐ Yes   ☐ No

Mortgage on this property: company: _____

loan # _____   monthly payment $_____

due on _____   ☐ automatic debit   ☐ paid by check

date

☐ Arranged

Date completed_____

I   ☐ do   ☐ do not   have other properties

I've listed them   ☐ on facing page

☐ on page(s) _____ at end of this book

Vehicle Information   **46**

Usual car key location_____

1)   Make   _____

Model   _____

License #   _____

I   ☐ do   ☐ don't   still owe money on this vehicle

Title location: _____

Car loan: company: _____

loan # _____   monthly payment $_____

due on _____   ☐ automatic debit   ☐ paid by check
             date

(if glove box is locked, here's how to open it):

2) Make _____

Model _____

License #   _____

I   ☐ do   ☐ don't   still owe money on this vehicle

Title location: _____

Car loan: company: _____

loan # _____   monthly payment $_____

             due on _____   ☐ automatic debit   ☐ paid by check
                        date

(if glove box is locked, here's how to open it):

I   ☐ do ☐ do not   have other vehicles.
I've listed them   ☐ on facing page
                              ☐ on page(s) _____ at end of this book

Contact and send death certificates to:

Equifax (to prevent identity theft) 888-298-0045   **47**

They will notify the two other credit agencies.

☐ Completed

Date completed_____

My bank(s)   **48**

I have bank accounts or investment accounts   ☐ Yes   ☐ No

Do they handle any monthly bill-pay arrangements ☐ Yes   ☐ No

Be sure to cancel debit cards

<u>Type of account</u>   <u>Bank Name</u>   /   <u>Account number</u>   .

Checking: _____ / _____

Phone: _____   Spoke with: _____

☐ Resolved

Date completed_____

Checking: _____ / _____

Phone: _____   Spoke with: _____

☐ Resolved

Date completed_____

Type of account   Bank Name   /   Account number

Savings: _____ / _____

     Phone: _____   Spoke with: _____

            ☐ Resolved

            Date completed_____

Savings: _____ / _____

     Phone: _____   Spoke with: _____

            ☐ Resolved

            Date completed_____

CD: _____ / _____

     Phone: _____   Spoke with: _____

            ☐ Resolved

            Date completed_____

CD: _____ / _____

     Phone: _____   Spoke with: _____

            ☐ Resolved

            Date completed_____

Type of account   Bank Name   /   Account number

Stocks: _____ / _____

        Phone: _____   Spoke with: _____

                                            ☐ Resolved

                                            Date completed_____

Stocks:_____ / _____

        Phone: _____   Spoke with: _____

                                            ☐ Resolved

                                            Date completed_____

Bonds: _____ / _____

        Phone: _____   Spoke with: _____

                                            ☐ Resolved

                                            Date completed_____

Bonds: _____ / _____

        Phone: _____   Spoke with: _____

                                            ☐ Resolved

                                            Date completed_____

Type of account   Bank Name   /   Account number

Other: _____ / _____

Phone: _____   Spoke with: _____

☐ Resolved

Date completed_____

Other: _____ / _____

Phone: _____   Spoke with: _____

☐ Resolved

Date completed_____

I ☐ do   ☐ do not   have other accounts

I've listed them   ☐ on facing page

☐ on page(s) _____ at end of this book

Credit Cards (Decide whether or not to cancel them)   **49**

(Cut them up as soon as they're canceled)

I have credit card(s)   ☐ Yes   ☐ No

card name &type   /   card number   / exp. date / CCV:

Personal: _____ / _____ / _____ / _____

☐ Cancelled

Date completed_____

Credit Cards (Continued)

| | card name & type | / | card number | / | exp. date | / | CCV: |

Personal: _____ / _____ / _____ / _____

☐ Cancelled

Date completed_____

Personal: _____ / _____ / _____ / _____

☐ Cancelled

Date completed_____

Business: _____ / _____ / _____ / _____

☐ Cancelled

Date completed_____

Business: _____ / _____ / _____ / _____

☐ Cancelled

Date completed_____

I keep my credit cards at these locations: _____

_____

I ☐ do ☐ do not   have other credit cards

   I've listed them   ☐ on facing page

                                   ☐ on page(s) _____ at end of this book

Annuities   **50**

   Do I have any annuities?   ☐ Yes ☐ No

   Firm/Contact Person: _____

   Phone: _____

   Email _____

   Street: _____

   City/State/ZIP _____

                              ☐ Contacted

                              Date completed_____

Retirement Accounts and IRAs   **51**

   Do I have any retirement accounts or IRAs? ☐ Yes ☐ No

   IRAs: custodian of the funds   /   account number   type   .

   _____ / _____ ☐ Trad. ☐ Roth

   website: _____

                              ☐ Contacted

                              Date completed_____

IRAs: <u>custodian of the funds</u>   /   <u>account number</u>   <u>type</u>

_____ / _____ ☐ Trad. ☐ Roth

website: _____

☐ Contacted

Date completed_____

Other Retirement Accounts:

.   <u>custodian of the funds</u>   /   <u>account number</u>   .

A. _____ / _____

website: _____

☐ Contacted

Date completed_____

B. _____ / _____

website: _____

☐ Contacted

Date completed_____

Other money or investment companies

Do I own a business or businesses?

☐ If yes, how many? _____   ☐ No   **52**

Name of my company: _____

It is a   ☐ corporation ☐ s-corp. ☐ LLC ☐ partnership ☐ sole prop.

_____

_____

_____

_____

I ☐ do ☐ do not   have other investments

    I've listed them   ☐ on facing page

                      ☐ on page(s) _____ at end of this book

Other Miscellaneous Income Sources (such as royalties, B&B, consulting fees...)   **53**

_____

_____

_____

_____

☐ Contacted

Date resolved_____

Contact Driver's license office so they can cancel my license.   **54**

I ☐ do   ☐ do not   have a current driver's license

State _____ number_____ exp. date_____

Keep a copy of the canceled driver's license in your records.

You may need it to close or access various accounts.

☐ Cancelled

Date completed_____

House and car insurance policies.   **55**

Keep the insurance until you've sold house(s) and car(s).

When you do cancel, ask that any unused premiums be returned.

☐ Cancelled

Date completed_____

House insurance (primary residence)

company _____ / policy #_____   **56**

Agent's name _____

Phone: _____

Email _____

☐ Cancelled

Date completed_____

House insurance (other)

company _____ / policy #_____   **57**

Agent's name _____

Phone: _____

Email _____

☐ Cancelled

Date completed_____

House insurance (rental property)

company _____ / policy #_____   **58**

Agent's name _____

Phone: _____

Email _____

☐ Cancelled

Date completed_____

Car insurance (vehicle #1)   **59**

company _____ / policy #_____

Agent's name _____

Phone: _____

Email _____

☐ Cancelled

Date completed_____

Car insurance (vehicle #2)

company _____ / policy #_____

Agent's name _____

Phone: _____

Email _____

☐ Cancelled

Date completed_____

I ☐ do ☐ do not have other vehicles. They are listed on the facing page or at the back of the book.

Terminate any other insurance policies and ask that any unused premiums be returned.

☐ Cancelled

Date completed_____

Drug Plan: **60**

company _____ / policy #_____

Agent's name _____

Phone: _____

Email _____

Street: _____

City/State/ZIP _____

☐ Cancelled

Date completed_____

Social Media platforms.   **61**

Delete the accounts (and yes, you need a death certificate to do that) **or memorialize them.**

These are the places where I have social media accounts **(be sure you've listed the login and passwords at Item #3)** :

Facebook   ☐ Yes   ☐ No

X (formerly Twitter)   ☐ Yes   ☐ No

Pinterest   ☐ Yes   ☐ No

Instagram   ☐ Yes   ☐ No

TikTok   ☐ Yes   ☐ No

Other   ☐ Yes   ☐ No

☐ Cancelled

Date completed_____

Cancel my email accounts.   **62**

You may want to use my email to reach the people I've asked you to contact.

Keep the account(s) running so you can see any messages that come in.

But there are many good reasons (like fraud and identity theft prevention) to shut down the accounts as soon as you don't need them anymore. Every email provider has their own process for closing an account. You can find out how to do it with a quick online search.

1) Email: _____

Username:_____

Password: _____

Security answer(s) _____

☐ Cancelled _____

Date completed_____

2) Email: _____

Username: _____

Password: _____

Security answer(s) _____

☐ Cancelled

Date completed_____

3) Email: _____

Username: _____

Password: _____

Security answer(s) _____

☐ Cancelled

Date completed_____

I ☐ do   ☐ do not   have other email accounts

I've listed them   ☐ on facing page

☐ on page(s) _____ at end of this book

Department of Voter Registration – be sure they know I'm dead.   **63**

You may need to take a death certificate to the Elections Office

address: _____

☐ Completed

Date completed_____

Internal Revenue Service (IRS) 800-829-1040   **64**

(press 1, then 2 to get a person. Good Luck!)

Take a deep breath! You are well more than half-way through this process.   **65**

Frequent buyer or frequent flyer programs   ☐ Yes   ☐ No   **66**

If yes, see if the points can be transferred to you or another family member.

These are the ones I have:

_____

☐ Cancelled

Date completed_____

_____

☐ Cancelled

Date completed_____

_____

☐ Cancelled

Date completed_____

I ☐ do   ☐ do not   have other frequent-whatever accounts

I've listed them   ☐ on facing page

☐ on page(s) _____ at end of this book

Meet with my current lawyer (Contact info is in item #28)   **67**

☐ Completed

Date completed_____

<u>Issues discussed:</u>

Take the will to probate court after: **68**

☐ You've notified beneficiaries and creditors
☐ You've inventoried assets and valuables
☐ Paid all the bills that are due
☐ Distributed the inheritances

What to submit to probate court

NOTE: This is a partial list of possibilities. **You can do an online search for the requirements in your state., but I strongly advise that you consult with your attorney (or mine) to be sure you have everything you'll need, which will (or may) include:**

☐ Death certificate
☐ Will / living trust documents
☐ List of heirs and beneficiaries (such as charities) with contact information
☐ Outstanding loan agreements
☐ Appraisal valuations for valuable items
☐ Financial statements
☐ Business statements
☐ Three years of tax returns (federal and state)
☐ Other known debts
☐ List of medical and funeral expenses

☐ Date delivered _____
☐ Court Date   _____

Date completed   _____

Once the probate process is complete, the case will be closed, and your term as executor will be officially over. That said, there ☐ are ☐ are not a few extra things you might want to consider. You'll find them in the next chapter.

Chapter 8 – What to Do Eventually

Decide whether or not to hold a **memorial service** at some later date after the funeral.   **69**

I kind of hope you ☐ do ☐ don't

    I ☐ will ☐ won't haunt you if you ignore these wishes.

    I ☐ have ☐ haven't put together some requests about this service. You'll find them **here**:

Call these people later (after a memorial service is scheduled)   **70**

    If there's no memorial service, then just contact them to let them know I'm dead.

This list is necessary because there are some people who don't have email addresses, but I still love them and want you to call them.

Name	Phone
_____ / _____	☐ Done
_____ / _____	☐ Done
_____ / _____	☐ Done
_____ / _____	☐ Done
_____ / _____	☐ Done

_____ / _____ ☐ Done

_____ / _____ ☐ Done

_____ / _____ ☐ Done

Notify these businesses later

NOTE: Some offices are notoriously hard to reach. The good news is that if I have an appointment scheduled, they'll usually text or email me ahead of time. Be sure you check my emails and texts, so you can reply / cancel the appointment / tell them I'm dead.

Specialist doctors, such as

Cardiologist _____   **71**

Phone _____

Email _____

Street _____

City/State/ZIP _____

☐ Notified Date _____

Chiropractor _____   **72**

Phon: _____

Email _____

Street _____

City/State/ZIP _____

☐ Notified Date _____

Children's pediatrician _____   **73**

    Phone _____

    Email _____

    Street: _____

    City/State/ZIP_____

            ☐ Notified Date _____

Podiatrist _____   **74**

    Phone: _____

    Email _____

    Street: _____

    City/State/ZIP_____

            ☐ Notified Date _____

Optometrist _____   **75**

    Phone_____

    Email _____

    Street _____

    City/State/ZIP_____

            ☐ Notified Date _____

☐ I don't wear glasses   ☐ I do wear glasses   # of pairs _____   Please donate them

They're located: _____

Dentist_____ **76**

    Phone_____

    Email_____

    Street:_____

    City/State/ZIP_____

               ☐ Notified Date _____

Dermatologist _____ **77**

    Phone_____

    Email_____

    Street_____

    City/State/ZIP_____

               ☐ Notified Date _____

Gynecologist _____ **78**

    Phone _____

    Email _____

    Street _____

    City/State/ZIP _____
            ☐ Notified   Date _____

Other Doctor _____ **79**

    Phone _____

    Email _____

    Street _____

    City/State/ZIP _____
            ☐ Notified   Date _____

Other doctor: _____ **80**

    Phone _____

    Email _____

    Street _____

    City/State/ZIP _____
            ☐ Notified   Date _____

Other doctor_____ **81**

Phone:_____

Email _____

Street: _____

City/State/ZIP_____

☐ Notified   Date _____

Other doctor_____ **82**

Phone_____

Email_____

Street_____

City/State/ZIP_____

☐ Notified   Date _____

I ☐ do   ☐ do not **have more doctors. If I do, I've listed them**

☐ on facing page

☐ on page(s) _____ at end of this book

My prescription meds are located:

Contact other businesses, such as:

Garbage removal _____   **83**

   (Cancel this AFTER you've cleaned out the house!)

Phone_____

Email_____

Street_____

City/State/ZIP_____

     ☐ Cancelled

     Date completed_____

Storage Facility clean it out before you cancel the contract.   **84**

Ask for a prorated refund of monthly fee.

Company: _____ Unit # _____

Phone: _____

Email _____

Street: _____

City/State/ZIP _____

     ☐ Cancelled

     Date completed_____

Hairdresser _____ **85**

    Phone: _____

    Email _____

             ☐ Contacted

             Date completed _____

High School/College Alumni Association(s)   **86**

    High School_____ class of _____

    Phone _____

    Email _____

    Street _____

    City/State/ZIP_____

             ☐ Notified

             Date completed_____

    College_____ class of _____

    Phone_____

    Email _____

    Street _____

    City/State/ZIP_____

             ☐ Notified

             Date completed_____

Other_____ class of _____

Phone_____

Email_____

Street_____

City/State/ZIP_____

☐ Notified

Date completed_____

I have other schools or professional organizations you'll need to contact ☐ Yes   ☐ No

I've listed them   ☐ on facing page

☐ on page(s) _____ at end of this book

Clear out my living space of all the personal things you & family members want.   **87**

☐ I have ☐ I have not   made a list of the things that you and others have requested.

You'll find the list here:_____

Arrange for a storage unit if necessary.

☐ Do ☐ Do not   give as much away as possible to _____ where they can
sell my things to help others.

☐ Completed

Date completed_____

Here are some suggestions as to what can be given away to what organization(s)

Death anniversary wishes   **88**

I ☐ do ☐ do not   want you to celebrate the anniversary of my death in a particular way.
   I ☐ don't care one way or the other. **Do whatever makes you happy**.

Here's what I'd prefer:

☐ light a candle ☐ say a prayer ☐ enjoy a special meal ☐ bake my favorite cookies

☐ dress up ☐ dress down ☐ go swimming ☐ hike in a park ☐ feed the birds

☐ other _____

Valuable items

                                                                                89

☐ I have   ☐ I do not have   valuables that will need to be appraised.
They include
☐ jewelry   ☐ furniture   ☐ collectibles
☐ crafts   ☐ weapons   ☐ china   ☐ silver
☐   fine art   ☐ other

☐ I have   ☐ I have not had them appraised.

☐ I had them appraised on _____, and the appraisal reports are located here:
                        date(s)

Here is a brief list of what to look for and where it/they are located:

- _____

- _____

- _____

- _____

- _____

- _____

- _____

                        ☐ Completed

                        Date completed_____

I have other items you'll need to consider   ☐ Yes   ☐ No

     I've listed them   ☐ on facing page

                        ☐ on page(s) _____ at end of this book

Arrange to sell my house and car(s).   **90**

Note: Don't be in too much of a hurry to do this. Take your time and do it right.

Primary residence

    Agency contracted with _____

    Phone _____

          ☐ Completed

          Date completed_____

Secondary residence

    Agency contracted with _____

    Phone_____

          ☐ Completed

          Date completed_____

Rental property

    Agency contracted with _____

    Phone _____

          ☐ Completed

          Date completed_____

Are there others?   ☐ Yes ☐ No

    I've listed them   ☐ on facing page

                 ☐ on page(s) _____ at end of this book

Vehicle #1

Where/How it's listed for sale: _____

Contact info: _____

☐ Completed

Date completed_____

Vehicle #2

Where/How it's listed for sale: _____

Contact info: _____

☐ Completed

Date completed_____

Cancel my passport   91

Do I have a passport?   ☐ Yes   ☐ No   Location:_____

You have a couple of options for how to deal with my passport. You do not have to return it; you can keep it as a memento, with the stamps on its pages reminding you of my past adventures. If you're worried about the possibility of identity theft, mail the passport to the federal government along with a copy of the death certificate and have it officially canceled. If you want the canceled passport returned, include a letter requesting that be done. Or you can request that they destroy the passport after it's been canceled.

☐ Did not mail it   ☐ Mailed it

Date mailed_____

Date completed_____

Complete an unclaimed property search for the decedent. (That would be me.)   **92**

This can be done via www.missingmoney.com

Don't know if there will be anything there, but one can never tell.

Note: I can help you out by doing the search myself ahead of time.

☐ I did such a search on _____   ☐ I did not do a search
                                    date
                              ☐ Completed

                              Date completed_____

Update your own estate plan to reflect the new situation with what you've   **93**

inherited from me.

                              ☐ Completed

                              Date completed_____

Buy another copy of this book so you can do the same for your   **94**

loved ones as I've done for you.

                              ☐ Completed

                              Date completed_____

Chapter 9 – If You Want to Go a Bit Further

This may be more than I want to prepare, or more than you want to do. If I don't write anything here, you're off the hook. If I HAVE filled this out, I'd truly appreciate your following through.

☐ I will   ☐ I will not   extract vengeance if you don't.

Please contact these special people with individual notes (which I've written here):   **95**

A. Name   _____

☐ Completed

Date completed_____

Phone: _____

Email   _____

Street: _____

City/State/ZIP   _____

Special words to say/write to them:

B. Name   _____

☐ Completed

Date completed_____

Phone: _____

Email   _____

Street: _____

City/State/ZIP   _____

Special words to say/write to them:

C. Name   _____

☐ Completed

Date completed_____

Phone: _____

Email   _____

Street: _____

City/State/ZIP   _____

Special words to say/write to them:

Last-minute stuff   **96**

Extra blank pages are included in this book for any additional notes you may need to record.

On the last two pages, you'll find an index so you can find any item easily. The numbers refer to the **ITEM NUMBERS IN THE RIGHT-HAND MARGIN** (like the 96 for last minute stuff), and the checkboxes are for the executor to mark when that item has been completed.

Chapter 10 – Closing Notes

Congratulations! You did it!

Whether you're the one who filled in all the blanks or the one who carried through with those wishes (or directives), you can be proud of your accomplishment.

This can't have been easy for either of you, but I hope you've gotten good value from the process.

Now it's time to keep on living.

Enjoy the rest of your journey.

--Fran

Notes

Notes (continued)

Notes (continued)

Notes (continued)

Index

For handy reference, check the box when you've completed the item

Index (continued)

For handy reference, check the box when you've completed the item